WE ARE DIFFERENT

by
Alex Hall

Minneapolis, Minnesota

Credits
Cover, © wavebreakmedia/Shutterstock; 4, © fizkes/Shutterstock; 5, © Distinctive Images/Shutterstock; 6L, © matimix/Shutterstock; 6R, © wavebreakmedia/Shutterstock; 7, © Monkey Business Images/Shutterstock; 8, © APIWAN BORRIKONRATCHATA/Shutterstock; 9, © Lopolo/Shutterstock; 10, © Sergey Novikov/Shutterstock; 11, © fizkes/Shutterstock; 12, © Ground Picture/Shutterstock; 13T, © Rawpixel.com/Shutterstock; 13B, © Roberto Galan/Shutterstock; 14L, © MIA Studio/Shutterstock; 14M, © Photographielove/Shutterstock; 14R, © Sutipond Somnam/Shutterstock; 15L, © PRM Photo/Shutterstock; 15M, © Creative Minds2/Shutterstock; 15R, © Roman Yanushevsky/Shutterstock; 16, © wavebreakmedia/Shutterstock; 17, © 1st footage/Shutterstock; 18, © Monkey Business Images/Shutterstock; 18R, © Monkey Business Images/Shutterstock; 19, © StockImageFactory.com/Shutterstock; 19B, © fizkes/Shutterstock; 20, © fizkes/Shutterstock; 21, © Olena Yakobchuk/Shutterstock; 22, © PeopleImages.com - Yuri A/Shutterstock; 23, © Kostiantyn Voitenko/Shutterstock.

Bearport Publishing Company Product Development Team
Publisher: Jen Jenson; Director of Product Development: Spencer Brinker; Editorial Director: Allison Juda; Editor: Cole Nelson; Editor: Tiana Tran; Production Editor: Naomi Reich; Art Director: Kim Jones; Designer: Kayla Eggert; Designer: Steve Scheluchin; Production Specialist: Owen Hamlin

Library of Congress Cataloging-in-Publication Data is available at www.loc.gov or upon request from the publisher.

ISBN: 979-8-89577-026-9 (hardcover)
ISBN: 979-8-89577-457-1 (paperback)
ISBN: 979-8-89577-143-3 (ebook)

© 2026 BookLife Publishing
This edition is published by arrangement with BookLife Publishing.

North American adaptations © 2026 Bearport Publishing Company. All rights reserved. No part of this publication may be reproduced in whole or in part, stored in any retrieval system, or transmitted in any form or by any means, electronic, mechanical, photocopying, recording, or otherwise, without written permission from the publisher. Bearport Publishing is a division of FlutterBee Education Group.

For more information, write to Bearport Publishing, 3500 American Blvd W, Suite 150, Bloomington, MN 55431.

CONTENTS

WE ARE CONNECTED 4
EVERYONE IS DIFFERENT 6
THE WAY WE LOOK 8
LANGUAGES 10
CULTURE 12
RELIGION 14
DISABILITIES 16
FAMILIES 18
GETTING ALONG WITH DIFFERENCES 20
WHY IT IS GOOD TO BE DIFFERENT 22
GLOSSARY 24
INDEX 24

WE ARE CONNECTED

The world is full of people. We are all connected in a society. Together, we can make sure everyone has what they need.

There are more than 8 billion people in the world.

WHAT COMMUNITIES ARE YOU PART OF?

Within our society, there are many different communities. These are groups that share things in common. Some communities are connected by what people in the group like or believe. There are communities of people with a shared history.

EVERYONE IS DIFFERENT

There are many things people have in common. But we all have our differences, too. Our interests, **personalities**, and talents are some of the things that make us **unique**.

What are some things that make you different?

All of these differences make our communities and societies stronger. What are some of the amazing ways we are different?

7

THE WAY WE LOOK

Everybody looks a little different. Some people are taller, and others are shorter. We have different skin colors. Our hair comes in different **textures**. We cannot change these things about ourselves.

What makes you look different from your best friend?

TWINS

Twins often look similar, but they can make choices about how to be different, too.

However, we can make some choices about the way we look. Picking the clothes we wear shows others a little bit about ourselves. So does how we choose to wear our hair.

LANGUAGES

There are many languages around the world. Most languages are spoken. But some use hand movements. These are called sign languages.

Some people who are deaf or hard of hearing use sign languages to **communicate**.

There are more than 7,000 languages around the world.

Communities often form around shared languages. Some people who live in different parts of the world speak the same language. They are connected even though they live far apart.

CULTURE

A community's **culture** is their set of goals, beliefs, and practices. Often, people of the same **ethnicity**, or whose families are historically from the same parts of the world, have a shared culture.

12

What is something you enjoy from your culture?

There are many different foods, art, music, and celebrations tied to cultures around the world. The way these things are a part of daily life also changes from one group to the next.

RELIGION

There are about 10,000 **religions** around the world. And there are even different branches within some of these religions. Each religion has its own set of beliefs and **traditions**.

I AM CHRISTIAN.

I AM BUDDHIST.

I AM SIKH.

Religion can shape many things about a person's daily life. People may take time to pray or celebrate special holidays. Some people do not eat certain foods because of their religion.

DISABILITIES

Some people have disabilities. This means they may experience the world differently than other people do. There are many kinds of disabilities.

Special tools, such as wheelchairs or hearing aids, help some people.

Disabilities can make it harder for people to do certain things, but that is only one part of who they are. We all have different strengths and challenges. No matter our abilities, we all deserve to be treated with **respect**.

FAMILIES

Families come in all shapes and sizes. You might have two moms, two dads, a mom and dad, or just one parent. Some people live together with their parents, grandparents, and cousins.

Who is in your family?

No matter what your family is like, the most important thing is that they care for you and support you.

19

GETTING ALONG WITH DIFFERENCES

Our differences mean that we may not always think the same way. Sometimes, this can lead to disagreements. That is okay! What we do next is important.

We may feel sad or angry when we do not agree with others.

How do you work through disagreements with others?

If we talk about our disagreements, we can learn what the other person is thinking and feeling. Take turns listening and speaking. You may start to see things from a different point of view.

21

WHY IT IS GOOD TO BE DIFFERENT

Around the world, people speak different languages, dress differently, and follow different religions. All of these things make us unique.

What kind of a society do you want to live in?

When we celebrate what makes each of us special, everyone is happier and healthier. This makes our society a nice place to be. It is better when we are all connected.

GLOSSARY

communicate to share information, ideas, or feelings

communities groups of people who live together or share something in common

culture the ideas, customs, and way of life shared by a group of people

ethnicity the background of where members of a person's family are from historically

personalities special habits and ways of behaving that make people who they are

religions sets of beliefs, often used to worship a god or gods

respect to consider something or someone important

textures the structures, feel, and appearances of things

traditions things that a group of people have done for many years

unique special and unlike anything or anyone else

INDEX

celebrations 13, 15, 23
communities 5, 7, 11–12
cultures 12–13
disabilities 16–17
ethnicity 12
families 12, 18–19
food 13, 15
religions 14–15, 22
society 4–5, 7, 23